S[redacted]and[redacted] Opera[redacted]

SAND OPERA

Standard Operating Procedure

SAND OPERA

PHILIP METRES

Alice James Books
Farmington, Maine
www.alicejamesbooks.org

Printed in the United States

11 10 9 8 7 6 5 4

Alice James Books are published by Alice James Poetry Cooperative, Inc., an affiliate of the University of Maine at Farmington.

Alice James Books
114 Prescott Street
Farmington, ME 04938
www.alicejamesbooks.org

Library of Congress Cataloging-in-Publication Data

Metres, Philip, 1970-
Sand opera / Philip Metres.
pages cm
ISBN 978-1-938584-09-1 (paperback)
1. Political poetry, American. I. Title.
PS3613.E887S26 2014
811'.6--dc23
2014010123

Alice James Books gratefully acknowledges support from individual donors, private foundations, the University of Maine at Farmington, and the National Endowment for the Arts.

ART WORKS.
arts.gov

Cover Art: "I am Baghdad II" courtesy of Ayad Alkadhi and Leila Heller Gallery New York

Contents

Illumination of the Martyrdom of St. Bartholomew 1

I. abu ghraib arias

The Blues of Lane McCotter 5
(echo /ex/): "In the name of God..." 6
Searching the Koran (Standard Operating Procedure) 7
(echo /ex/): "*In the beginning...*" 8
The Blues of Javal Davis 9
(echo /ex/): "next day..." 10
Public Address/Ghost Soldiers 11
(echo /ex/): "his name is G..." 12
The Blues of Charles Graner 13
(echo /ex/): "On the third day..." 14
Handling the Koran (Standard Operating Procedure) 15
(echo /ex/): "First the man..." 16
Document Exploitation (Standard Operating Procedure) 17
(echo /ex/): "*Now these are the generations...*" 18
The Blues of Lynddie England 19
(echo /ex/): "me..." 20
The Blues of Ken Davis 21
(echo /ex/): "Now I am what I saw..." 22
MUSLIM BURIAL (Standard Operating Procedure) 23
(echo /ex/): "*And it came to pass...*" 24
The Blues of Joe Darby 25
(echo /ex/) 26

II. first recitative

Woman Mourning Son 29
Recipe from the Abbasid 30
Home Sweet Home 33
The Iraqi Curator's PowerPoint 34
Black Site (Exhibit Q) 39
Asymmetries 40
Salaam Epigrams 42
War Stories 43

III. hung lyres

"The new theory: not to praise too much…" 47
"When the bombs fell, she could barely raise…" 48
"you mute you without openings…" 49
"*Is the ear…*" 50
"In the cell of else…" 52
"this is the air we script to lips…" 53
"I had no names to blazon their tender…" 54
"She asks, *is that man crying…*" 55
"What does it mean, I say." 56

IV. second recitative

Breathing Together 59
Testimony (after Daniel Heyman) 60
When I Was a Child, I Lived as a Child, I Said to My Dad 62

Black Site (Exhibit I) 67
Love Potion #42 68
Saddam's Fingerprints 69
Etruscan Cista Handle 70
Black Site (Exhibit M) 73
A Toast (for Nawal Nasrallah) 74
Cell/(ph)one (A simultaneity in four voices) 76

v. homefront/removes

"I hear it, at times, even in the wind." 81
"*was taken was rapidly…*" 82
"What consequence is a body." 83
"*tried hanging myself…*" 84
"I was planning my lesson on imagery…" 85
"*taken to outside court…*" 86
"In the wake of." 87
"*I suspended upside…*" 88
"You look at me / looking at you." 89
"*so I could pass the time…* " 90
"As if, somehow, I were responsible." 91
<hover to see video> 92
"On the flight overseas…" 93
"*I did not know my…*" 94

Compline 97

Notes 101

Also by Philip Metres

Poetry:
A Concordance of Leaves (chapbook)
abu ghraib arias (chapbook)
Ode to Oil (chapbook)
To See the Earth
Instants (chapbook)
Primer for Non-Native Speakers (chapbook)

Translation:
I Burned at the Feast: Selected Poems of Arseny Tarkovsky
Compleat Catalogue of Comedic Novelties: Poetic Texts of Lev Rubinstein
Catalogue of Comedic Novelties: Selected Poems of Lev Rubinstein
A Kindred Orphanhood: Selected Poems of Sergey Gandlevsky

Criticism:
Come Together: Imagine Peace
Behind the Lines: War Resistance Poetry on the American Homefront Since 1941

Acknowledgments

Grateful acknowledgment for publishing versions of these poems is due to *Banipal* (UK), *Diode*, *FIELD*, *Indiana Review*, *Kenyon Review Online*, *The Massachusetts Review*, *Matter*, *Mizna*, *Narrative*, *New Letters*, *New Orleans Review*, *Ostrich Review*, *POEM: International English Language Quaterly* (UK), *Poetry*, *Seneca Review*, *Publication of the Modern Language Association (PMLA)*, and *World Literature Today (WLT)*. Thanks as well to the anthologies *Come Together: Imagine Peace* (Bottom Dog Press, 2008), *Eating the Pure Light: Homage to Thomas McGrath* (The Backwaters Press, 2009), *The New American Poetry of Engagement: A 21st Century Anthology* (McFarland & Company, 2012), *Obsession: An Anthology of Sestinas* (Dartmouth, 2014), and *With Our Eyes Wide Open: Poems of the New American Century* (West End Press, 2014) for reprinting a number of these poems.

Selections prose sections from "Homefront/Removes" were published as "Home/Front," which won the Anne Halley Prize for best poem by *Massachusetts Review* (2011). One of the sections appeared as a broadside.

Thanks to Sommer Browning and Tony Mancus at Flying Guillotine Press for publishing *abu ghraib arias* as a chapbook (2011), which won the Arab American Book Award for poetry in 2012. The first version of the chapbook featured a cover made from recycled army uniforms, thanks to Chris Arendt and the Combat Paper Project.

Thanks to the National Endowment for the Arts, the Community Partnership for Arts and Culture (Creative Workforce Fellowship), Cuyahoga Arts & Culture, the Ohio Arts Council, and John Carroll University for grants in support of the writing of this work. The Creative Workforce Fellowship is a program of the Community Partnership for Arts and Culture. The Fellowship program is supported by the residents of Cuyahoga County through a public grant from Cuyahoga Arts & Culture.

Thanks to Rebecca Black, Hayan Charara, Sarah Gridley, Anna Meek, and Mary Weems for their extensive remarks on the manuscript. Thanks as well to Kazim Ali, Danny Caine, Michael Croley, Ian Demsky, Michael Dumanis, Fady Joudah, Marilyn Hacker, Chris Kempf, Dave Lucas, E.J. McAdams, Mark Nowak, Radius of Arab American Writers, Inc. (RAWI), and Maria Smith and the Cleveland Nonviolence Network for your encouragement. For opening spaces.

Thanks as well to Justin Petropoulos for creating renditions of Bashmilah's hand drawings of black sites.

Thanks to everyone at Alice James Books—especially Carey Salerno, Stephen Motika, Alyssa Neptune, Mary Austin Speaker, Julia Bouwsma, and Meg Willing—for making this happen.

And most importantly, thank you to Amy Breau, to whom this work is dedicated, for her constant companionship, her careful reading, her nurturing of our children Adele and Leila, and her invitation to a greater opening.

...it took the war to teach it, that you were responsible for everything you saw as you were for everything you did. The problem was that you didn't always know what you were seeing until later, maybe years later, that a lot never made it in at all, it just stayed there in your eyes.
—Michael Herr, *Dispatches*

If the whole body were an eye, where would the hearing be?
—1 Corinthians 12:17

Illumination of the Martyrdom of St. Bartholomew

from the dried hide of calves
carved & sewn in quires

they bend & tend to him / as if
tailors or healers & not rending

skin from limb / their eyes
narrowing knives / he balances

naked on ankle / a single
arm aloft as if in flight

from body's scything / O wholly
gold-haloed & yet-membered head

soothe the eye in which I am
thrown / hand without shield /

scissored out hymn / & if
the body's flayed & displayed

in human palms / & human skin
scrolled open / the body still dances

& if the flesh is the text
of God / bid a voice to rise /

& rise again

I.

abu ghraib arias

The Blues of Lane McCotter

four Iraqis at the gate
all of them missing
their hands or their
[redacted] story

under Saddam their arms
[redacted] had been
[redacted] said
they knew they were

buried on the grounds
they wanted to uncover
those bones for proper
[redacted]

four Iraqis [redacted]
I could not grant
access on account
[redacted]

[redacted] one could enter
[redacted] start taking pictures
[redacted]

they removed their hands
[redacted] I watched as night
[redacted] the rest of them

(echo /ex/)

In the name of God I swear to God everything I witnessed everything I am talking about. I am not saying this to gain any material thing, and I was not pressured to do so by any forces. I will not talk about what happened when I was in jail before, because they did not ask me, but it was very bad. They stripped me of my clothes, even my underwear. They gave me women's underwear that was rose color with flowers in it and they put the bag over my face. One of them whispered in my ear "today I am going to fuck you," *thy name shall be* and he said this in Arabic. Whoever was with me experienced the same thing…cuffed my hands with irons behind my back to the metal of the window, to the point that my feet were on the ground and I was hanging there for about five hours just because I asked about the time, because I wanted to pray…took all my clothes and took the underwear and he put it over my head. After he released me I don't know if they took a picture of me because they beat me so bad I lost

Searching the Koran (Standard Operating Procedure)

thereby reducing the friction over searching

will avoid handling or touching

may or may not require a language

to open

pages in an upright manner (as if reading

random

turn will be turned

see the pages

both ends

the book is

contours or protrusions

binding

the binding

(echo /ex/)

In the beginning I was there for 67 days of

[redacted] I saw myself *on the face*

of the deep *And the darkness he called Night*

And Graner released

my hand from the door and he cuffed my hand in the back.

I did not do anything [redacted] hit me hard on my

[redacted] cuffed me to the window of the room

a firmament in the midst of

[redacted] the first days of Ramadan

[redacted] came with two boys naked and [redacted] cuffed

together face to face and Graner was beating them and

[redacted] were watching and taking

pictures from top and bottom [redacted]

our image [redacted] *dominion*

every creeping thing female soldiers laughing

don't know their names

The Blues of Javal Davis

stay open about drawing
an opinion [redacted]
[redacted] from
the comforts of your living

room watching CNN
if you were actually on
the other side of CNN
fighting for your life pretty

much on our own working
seven days straight ducked
heads when mortars fell
slept seven to a cell

told to bang cans throw
cold slam doors blare Heavy
Metal all hours but prisoners
[redacted] air guitar

I blared "Hip Hop Hooray"
till they began to bob their heads
and then I played Country
they said Allah Allah cut it off

Country drove them crazy
CNN says we're some dumb
poor kids from Garbagecan USA
it didn't turn out to be that way

(echo /ex/)

next day

a blanket *of skins*

the door opened

G was there

and let them have

the chair until the chair was broken

and breathed a miracle I lived

new guard wears glasses

I saw things no one would see

then your eyes shall be opened

father and son

his father naked

into the toilet "go take it and eat it"

and your eyes shall be

dogs G brought the dogs

Public Address/Ghost Soldiers

the importance of keeping accurate and complete

don't ask you don't ask you don't you
just say yes sir when they say

keep accurate and complete

intelligence value the prisoner extracted

is dead we weren't here have a good
day we say yes sir they were we don't

to play the call to prayer

the prisoner

in a calm clear voice

(echo /ex/)

his name is G

"Do you believe in

my broken

ark which he had made

I lost

I lost

G came and laughed

lo, in her mouth

it will break again

arms behind

broken because I can't

sever pain

X

X the hard site

while the earth remaineth

some pictures

shall not cease

The Blues of Charles Graner

the Christian in me
knows it's wrong
but the corrections
officer in me can't
help but love
making a grown man
piss himself

(echo /ex/)

On the third day G came

made me no clothing

wires on my fingers penis

bag over my head

saying electric

flash of the camera

in the garden

and I fell down

thy voice

made me stand made me

white chair high in the air

till thou return unto the ground

I woke up to sleep

Handling the Koran (Standard Operating Procedure)

avoid handling or touching

a language specific

to open the one cover with one hand

in an upright manner (as if reading

not every page is to be

clearly see the pages

reverence

two hands at all times

Handle as if it were fragile

delicate art

(echo /ex/)

First the man A

stripped cursed

pushed the first on top of the others

A refused G

into your hand are they delivered

ordered to stand

testicles with gloves hand-

cuffed

water

G pouring water

screaming "my heart"

And the waters shall *flood* *all flesh*

all this beating

to stitch the string the needle

the operation succeeded

Document Exploitation (Standard Operating Procedure)

clearly and legibly skip lines

as close as possible

to the original

tense and person the writer used

Don't translate proverbs word for word

Don't translate poems word for word

ask someone for help

the meaning of some words

further clarify [redacted]

names [redacted]

look [redacted]

up the letter you [redacted] started

to [redacted] translate letters, not [redacted]

analyze them

(echo /ex/)

Now these are the generations

of the hardsite

animals not humans

write words on our buttocks

what it means

no clothes   no mattresses   dogs

naked   night   take the negative from the night

guard and you will find everything I said was true…

after their tongues

white man   white glasses

ordered us to stroke

in his mouth

my penis with a pen

this night   like 1000 nights

The Blues of Lynddie England

[G] played me
I guess I was blind
by love
maybe it was

[   ]

for documentation
maybe it was
for his own
amusement

[   ]

I don't know
what was going through
his head
but he took it

[   ]

it shows
he has power
over me
anything he asked

[   ]

he knew
I would do

(echo /ex/)

me

he me he

he me

I he

he he he

he me I

he he he

I I G

me me I

I He He

I I

I

The Blues of Ken Davis

and I remember calling
home that night and saying
I can't take this anymore

if this is what we're going
to do if this is what we've become
then I'm done

they say talk to a chaplain
they say it's all your perception
and every night it's amazing

because you're lying there
no matter how much music you play
no matter how loud you turn it up

you still can hear [redacted]

(echo /ex/)

Now I am what I saw

naked and

tied

G

lift up his eyes cuffed together

I saw [redacted] fucking a kid

Behold all the doors with sheets

I
saw [redacted]

the cell *I will go down now*

on the other side sheets again on the doors G

[redacted]

the phosphoric light

for God's help [redacted]

in his ass *dust and ash*

standing under

I was there without me seeing

MUSLIM BURIAL (Standard Operating Procedure)

like sandalwood

the whole body a prayer folded

folded

(SIDE VIEW)

BOTTOMLESS BURIAL VAULT

(CONCRETE)

→

DIRECTION TOWARD MECCA

TRENCH

BODY OF DECEASED

---

enshrouding “O Allah, forgive this deceased”

(echo /ex/)

And it came to pass

he was opening

feet on my neck   feet on my head

here I am

out of the room   inside the
room

Abide here

the broom

the glowing finger   until I was

laid upon   *the altar*

the stick that he always carries inside

me

Here I am

lifted up

I saw inside   *a burnt offering*

pictures of me   instances

The Blues of Joe Darby

I laughed at first I did
not know what I was looking at
a bunch of bodies bending over
a pyramid of tumbling

They call me bulls-eye they call me traitor

the pictures were taken
the pictures I gave them
now they are everywhere and I
can't go home again

They call me walking dead call me waking night

I dream they stand on naked
boxes again they back on each other's
backs again they bloody mouth from flinch
of dogs they hands on sandbagged heads

call me talking dead call me waking eye

I gun to sleep again I closet night
no sleep but I would give them up again
I close exposed I wake and listen
I would give them up again

(echo /ex/)

“ , , ,

, .

,

.

,

. “

.”

. ,

.

, .

.

. .

.

:

:

[ ] [

] .

.”

II.

first recitative

Woman Mourning Son
—Najaf

I pull up the blinds, they screech in retreat,
mad grackles beaking for space on the lawn.
I flip open the news and she flutters out,
trailing the blot of her shadow. I yawn,

her mouth yawns and yawns. Like wings, her chador
unfurls over a bare, bleached street. She looks
almost like she's flying, one leg cut off
by the photo. The shape of her shadow's

an F-16, the flat plane of her hand
the jet nose, the other hand a missile
tucked so gently beneath the wing. And now
the blot of that shadow's a flailing bat,

a ragged flag—this black-clad woman's hands
open and skyward, as if she wants to vault
the blot of this shadow. From above, it looks
just like whirling, a waltz with no one

but chadors and shadows. Now she's lost
her face in the ink. The road is a white
sheet. Somewhere someone's hands danced
over a keyboard to deliver the ordnance.

Recipe from the Abbasid

Skin & clean a fat, young sheep & open it
like a door, a port city hosting overseas guests

& remove its stomach. In its interior, place
surveyors in exploratory khaki, a stuffed goose

& in the goose's belly, a stuffed hen, & in the hen,
machine gun nests, C rations, grenades, a stuffed

pigeon, & in the pigeon's belly, a stuffed thrush,
& in the thrush's belly, contractual negotiations

& subtle threats, all sprinkled with sauce. Sew the slit
into a smile, dispatch handshakes. Add Chevron,

Exxon, Texaco, Shell. Place the sheep in the oven
& leave until this black slimy stuff, excretion

of the earth's body, is crispy on the outside,
& ready for presentation.

I climbed inside, they closed
the hatch. Sat there thinking,
this is such a little hole,
and my love was so much
bigger than me. And: this hole
was where he died, where they drove
through a berm, into the Tigris
They told me about scratch marks.
I tried not to look, but I couldn't
stop thinking about him trying
to scratch his way out, the tank
filling with water. You take that last
breath, can only hold it so long
before you have to breathe again

Home Sweet Home

When the Abu Ghraib photos first came out, I was in Afghanistan capturing insurgents and bringing them to the Interrogation Facility in Bagram. We gathered intel tying M, a former Taliban and judge in the Ghazni Province, to many murders including the torture, rape and burning alive of little
children in front of
their parents so we
searched his office and
found ledgers, lists
of deceased people and
houses he
stole he was tied
to deaths of our
own soldiers help
remembering remember
the terrible stench of
this man I
remember talking
with people who
wanted only to know where their relatives' bones were buried. But M was eventually released. He was a murderer, but we didn't detain murderers, only terrorists and insurgents. I remember lying on my cot at night and looking up at the ceiling and thinking I had looked directly in the eyes of evil and could do nothing about it. I could do nothing about it.

The Iraqi Curator's PowerPoint

You can see the footprints around the hole
The Iraqi Curator said. They smashed the head
Because they could not lift it from its base,
This statue of Nike. It's still missing.
And this is *Umma Al-Ghareb*, my dig site.
The Mother of Scorpions, it means. *Y'anni*,

Next slide: more damage by looters. If the eyes
Are gems, they will be made into holes.
If the skin is gold, goodbye. Now this is a sight:
The bodies too heavy, so they took the heads
Of these terracotta lions. A slide is missing
Here. What I ask you is this: base

What you believe on what you can almost see.
For example: you hear the dogs bay
From the outskirts of the city. They head
Wherever they smell flesh. My eyes
Still see buildings that now are holes.
What you see is not what is missing.

Next slide. I'd heard that Etana, missing
For years, was in Damascus. Then in Beirut.
Then, I got a call from an art friend, a whole
Continent away. Does it have a scratch at the base
Of his hand and along his chest I said he said yes
Of course I said and it is headless

And writing on the shoulder beneath no head
And he said yes and yes the right arm missing

And I said my God I said John take my eyes
And let me see. I was blind and now had sight
Though I could not see it. This is the basis
Of art, *sadiki*. There's something beyond the hole

Which each must face. Missile sites. Army bases.
The hole in the ground where thousands climbed
Into sky. Missing heads of state. Eyes.

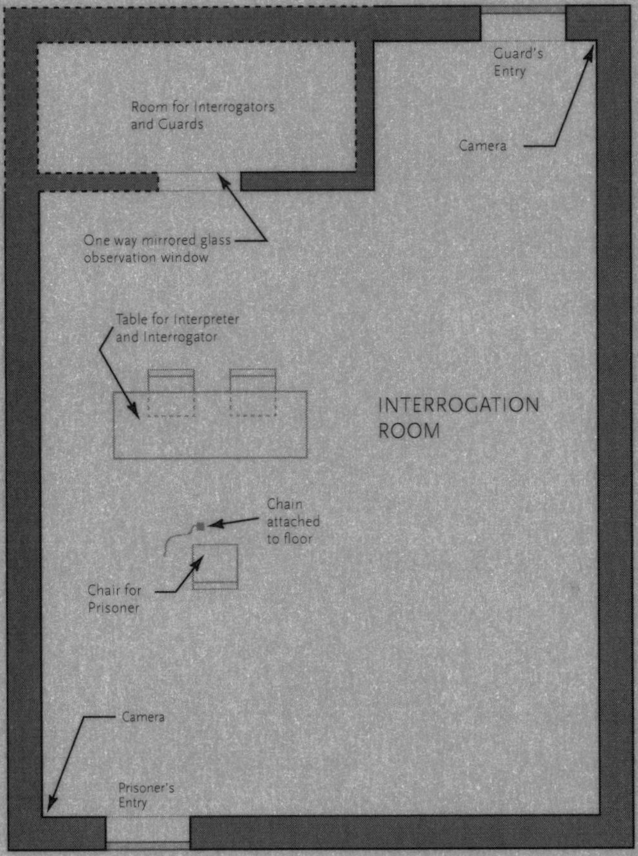
Room for Interrogators
and Guards
Guard's
Entry
Camera
One way mirrored glass
observation window
Table for Interpreter
and Interrogator
INTERROGATION
ROOM
Chain
attached
to floor
Chair for
Prisoner
Camera
Prisoner's
Entry

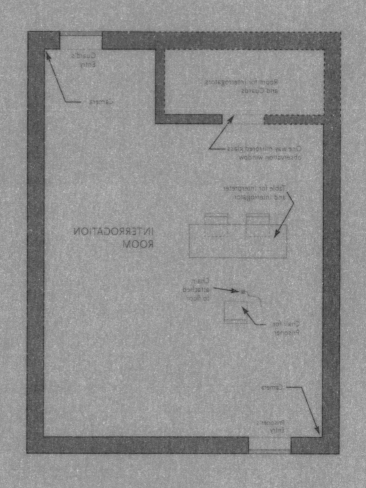

Black Site (Exhibit Q)

so I could

pass the time

they also gave me

a Rubik's Cube

Asymmetries

Longing to grasp the familiar, names
          against the anonymous
appendages & naked flesh, a nipple the eye
          could nuzzle, to hide in
dark islands of hair, I near the photo—

          as if the body erotic
could shield against the camera's scalpel.
          In its distance, the bodies
without faces line a riverbank, shade
          into some darker shadow,

obeying the desire of gravity. I'm thinking
          of Iraq, how they lay out
each disinterred nest of femurs & ribs
          on separate sackcloths,
trying to punctuate the run-on sentence.

          After making love, once,
you said every face, split in half, fit
          so precariously, so comically,
we spent the next half hour shading one side
          of our faces in the mirror,

then the other. This world is centaur: half
          daydream, half nightmare,
not knowing if we're awake or dreaming.
          Wandering the gallery, we drift
onto an imagined balcony

& gape at the traffic
of bodies jamming the crossroads, im
-mobile sculpture of
pure fact, dangling odd-angled & earth
-bound us.

Salaam Epigrams

—for Leila

You trail a comet's tail.
Everything you do quotes you.

O well overflowing, tell.
Broken vessel you, don't heal.
Stream of grief: blessing.

You awaken in the wake
of a sentence half-written,

the missing past tense
cordoned by comma.

Star jiggered from sky
to green ground, you
beeline toward its bloom.

Apostrophe of a womb—
fetal you—and the line you will become.

War Stories

The fitful sleep of steak and silver. We
man the monitors of dreaming, on this outpost
of fatherhood. The battlements of silence.
A friend opens a bottle of red. We've lived
in this dome so long it seems like freedom.
We know the crackle of distant gunfire
heightened by stereo, the plith of dust,
each stray bullet pirouetting in slo-mo.
Our fathers and brothers wear the flak jacket
of medal and shrapnel. We don the softness
of palms, the odor of diaper wipes. Somewhere
outside, someone's brother's buried
a box he won't tell us where. Inside the box
is. We gird the landscape in the soundtrack
of earbuds, but inside the box is a baby
radio hissing. Inside is the rattle unjawed.
In the rings of our suburbs, outside the zone
of ground zeroes. The baby is stirring, not
crying. Inside the well of our glasses,
the smutch of discernable breathing.

III.

hung lyres

@

The new theory: not to praise too much, lest the child lose her inner sense of what pleasures, the listening tuned inward.

In silence before sleep, looking up to her ceiling, four years in her mind, she says: *someone is telling the story of our life.*

I see her great-grandmother in her brown eyes, in her roil of curls.

I don't know who it is.

In the woods of her wander, she.

They will be telling it our whole life.

@

When the bombs fell, she could barely raise
her pendulous head, wept shrapnel

until her mother capped the fire
with her breast. She teetered

on the highwire of herself. She
lay down & the armies retreated, never

showing their backs. When she unlatched
from the breast, the planes took off again.

Stubborn stars refused to fall…

@

you mute you without openings

enwombed you greedy to eat the fruit of light
to swallow elixirs of sound

marooned you in that watery egg that mother
voice a constant hum above

this is the air you could & ample be
everyone waking to sirens

the arc & com
motion of glass released from its bottle

this is aria of nightfall that sets the anvil
to tremble the temple behind the temples

when you emerged not mouth or fingers but cries
& whorls & folds to hold sound in

the first thing I saw was your ear

@

Is the ear

no name to blazon
the curve

Is the leaning in

we inherit: auricle
bloom

Is the ear

oracle
drum

Is the listing

vestibule
elliptical

Is the ear

host a motion labyrinth
incus

Hung lyre

my child not yet
your silk wind

Is the ear

    too soon   to bend

Burning

Your flexible   ocean

@

In the cell of else / in the pitch-white
someone's hands shackled between ankles

in the nights & *sunny days keeping the clouds*
shaking the rib cage & no way

to keep the music from entering & breaking
the bodies hit / Let the bodies hit the / Barney

is a dinosaur / this is the touching without being
touched / this is the being without

silence / *from our imagination* / in wave upon
wave / in a shipping container & *I love you*

in a box of shock *you love me* / in a cemented
dream / *we're a happy family* /

with a great big hug and chains that leave no mark
Won't you say you love me too?

@

this is the air we script to lips / air we usher in lungs / that ushers us
in / this is the air / there is no other / we unseal & key / the same air /
hair of the fathers / shoulder of the mothers / air of laughter & air
of slaughter / air / of wrecks & reliquaries / of wasp & papyrus
barbed wire & hung / lyres & this is the air we draw in / air we expel
sphere that spires in us / spears us into us / stories we find ourselves
in / the middle of something / a building we did not build
& this is the air of ozone & benzene / that quickens the blood /
clarifies the eye / this is the air / there is no other / nesting in us /
then beaked & breaking / a sudden flutter / ring / out of us /
this is the air we gather / there is no other / lower / nature / field
this the clearing / this the threshing / floor the flesh's door / unseen
seething song that fills the nautilus that the little hammer wields
to drum / aria of the air sculpting the thinking bone

@

I had no names to blazon their tender
curves, their riverine curves

so took the ones we inherit: auricle
to name the human bloom—

what does it mean, amputee?

lobed trumpet that listens to the oracle
of cymballed world: canal & drum

vestibule to the oceanic home
where windows are elliptical & circular

is there such a thing as "orphan"?

& we host a motion labyrinth, a squid.
Maleus, incus, stapes. Cover your ears

dear child, your cartilage is not yet hard—
it's too soon to know to hear is to bend.

Your silk purses will sow the wind.
Your flexible shells haul their own ocean.

@

She asks: *is that man crying*
or singing? How should I answer?

War takes him in its fingers,
raises his body, a punctured bone

flute, to its lips, and breathes
the living dust
                    to dust alone—

this is the air we scull
air of ancestors & ashpits

just five, the child's baptized into this
unhappiness:
            she corrects the voices

she hears butcher
the name of the country she's never

seen—*it's "ear-rock,"*
not "eye-rack."

@

What does it mean, I say. She says, it means
to be quiet, just by yourself. She says, there's

a treasure chest inside. You get to dig it out.
Somehow, it's spring. Says, will it always

rain? In some countries, I say, they are
praying for rain. She asks, why do birds sing?

In the dream, my notebook dipped in water,
all the writing lost. Says, read the story again.

But which one? That which diverts the mind
is poetry. Says, you know those planes

that hit those buildings? Asks, why do birds sing?
When the storm ends, she stops, holds her hands

together, closes her eyes. What are you doing?
I'm praying for the dead worms. Says, listen:

IV.

second recitative

Breathing Together

Bear with me. I want to explain why it took so long, the strange and hard ways this mss. hit me. Weeks ago, a close friend who worked for the State Department killed himself, apparently leaping from the Taft Bridge. It was shocking, but also unbelievable—truly, we did not believe it at first. P— was in no way suicidal. He and I had had a conversation where he scoffed at those who ended their lives. He'd seen a lot of godawful things, had interviewed hundreds of Holocaust survivors, and felt it was his duty to bear witness. No obit was released for a long time, the family wasn't talking, and no police reports of a suicide on that day. I tracked down that the news came through a woman who had been staying with P—. It sounds like a conspiracy movie, but on the day of his death, two federal officers came to the apartment at 6 am and interviewed him privately for an hour. She was asked to leave. When she returned, the officers confiscated P—'s home computer. They made plans for dinner, and he left for work—the last anyone saw him. P— had been interviewing people in Iraq and Afghanistan, soldiers and detainees. He was a research phenom, intensely moral—self-righteously so. Perhaps he stumbled onto information he shouldn't have and was considering releasing it.... We're all being cautious about how we talk about this. You don't have to say anything back about it, but I wanted you to know a little of the story.

Testimony (after Daniel Heyman)

I sit in a hotel room and draw this Iraqi.
The question is: how to fill the frame
With each etched face, each bound body.
They stripped the father and son, this man says,
[redacted]
They made the father strike the son.

Son and father   the stripped they, I write.
I listen as I draw and try to disappear
And make the father strike his son
[redacted]
While I draw and try to disappear
Scratches turn into words, [redacted].

Hovering in words around his unbound head,
Like a hovering mother or torturer
Scratches turn into words, [redacted]:
They could not make son hit the father.
[redacted]
I sketch with a stylus on a copper plate

Father [redacted] hit son   make not   could they
[redacted]
How *they made the father dig a hole*
The words scratched backwards, as in a mirror.
And *they made the son get into the hole*.

How they made the father dig a hole
I have to write very quickly

How they made the son get into the hole
And made the father bury him up to his neck.
I have to write very quickly
So I do not lose the [redacted]

And made the father bury him up to his neck
And later ride him like a donkey.
So I do not lose [redacted]
Each etched face, each bound body
And later ride him like a donkey—
I sit in a hotel room and draw this Iraqi.

When I Was a Child, I Lived as a Child, I Said to My Dad

Saint Paul was a jackass, my father muttered,
keystroking his tank into position in *The Mother*

of All Tank Battles. I turned back to the screen,
maneuvering pixilated tanks. Each arrow key

altered trajectory, each cursor tap a tank blast. Fast-
forward two decades: in a cubicle outside Vegas,

Jonah joysticks his Predator above Afghanistan,
drone jockey hovering above a house on computer screen.

He knows someone's inside. Is it his target? Who else
inside—cooking, crawling—will not outrun his digital will?

He is cross hairs and shaking frame. Stone implosion.
He watches the collapse replay on-screen, then

heads home. Pizza. Diaper rash. Removes a thumb
from his toddler's sleeping mouth. Again, no sleep.... Our game's

quaintly obsolete. On mailboxes around our neighborhood,
our beagle would sign his line of piss, which said: it's good

to be alive and eating meat. He was adding to the map
our eyes can't see, nor throats can speak. Our shield and our help

at Great Lakes Naval Base, my father imagined permutations
of disaster. We were Region Five. Coordinates run,

scenarios conceived, New Madrid fault lines, the possible
flood of Des Plaines, a tornado's blinding spiral

rolling its dozer across the plain. No preparing for it,
just to pick up what remained. If a nuclear bomb hit

Chicago, the epicenter *here*, he'd draw concentric circles
radiating, a pebble disturbing the mirror of a lake. Each circle

meant a slower death. Between us and them, the Wall
was a mirror reflecting us and nothing beyond. The whole

world was what the mirror hung upon. He showed me how
to hold a blade, how to watch my reflection for every nick, how

to cut my face without bleeding. I bled. I hooked my glasses
over teenaged ears. Outside, the blur of lawn became grass,

each blade stabbing upward to light. I thought I knew
we see as through a glass, darkly.... My frames have narrowed

to lenses eye-sized. My myopia grows. To see
what's happening, I open a laptop, lean into the screen:

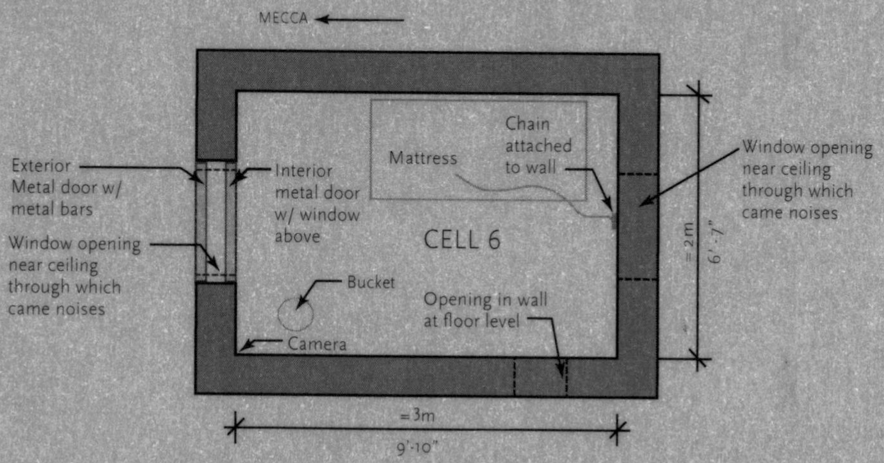
MECCA
Exterior Metal door w/ metal bars
Window opening near ceiling through which came noises
Interior metal door w/ window above
Mattress
Chain attached to wall
Window opening near ceiling through which came noises
CELL 6
Bucket
Opening in wall at floor level
Camera
=2m
6'-7"
=3m
9'-10"

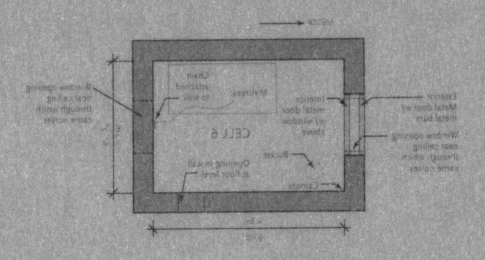

Black Site (Exhibit I)

Whenever I saw

a fly in my cell

I was filled

with joy

though I wished for it

to slip under the door

so it would not be

imprisoned itself

Love Potion #42

Before you, I slept on a bayonet.
Bided my time in clothing. Neither experience
nor innocence kept me

from bleeding. Before you, I held
an invisible sign: *please touch this abyss.*
How pleasing to have you sieve me

through your lungs, leave me essential
dregs and seeds. Since there's no place
a grain of sand cannot hide, deserts

and strands now travel the world
with us, in shoes. Let me kind you in two
tongues. *Habibti*, two decades ago,

we fell off a cliff, each holding a wing,
each holding a hand, and have yet to land.

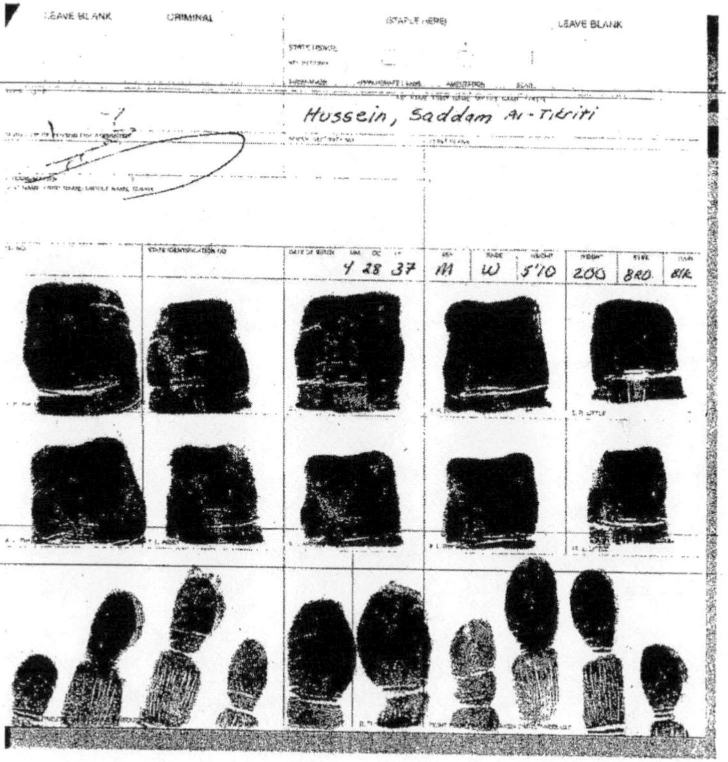
LEAVE BLANK

CRIMINAL

STAPLE HERE

LEAVE BLANK

Hussein, Saddam Al-Tikriti

Date of Birth	Sex	Race	Height	Weight	Eyes	Hair
4 28 37	M	W	5'10	200	BRO	BLK

Etruscan Cista Handle

How peaceful he looks, the gates of his face
now shut for good, facing the ground. His body's

hoisted horizontal, his arms embrace
the air, his penis a slack finger of gravity.

Two winged soldier-angels must stoop, stagger
to cradle his naked inhuman weight.

Their heads torqued, as if listening to the lead
of the body, they bear it in bent tender shoulders,

in the balked leaning and strain of their gait,
and struggle against falling. Their maker is dead.

And still the war continues, though it takes
other names. Sarpedon bronzed not breathing, the angels

bronze stumbling, all burned into a single handle.
To open the jewelry box, you have to grasp the corpse.

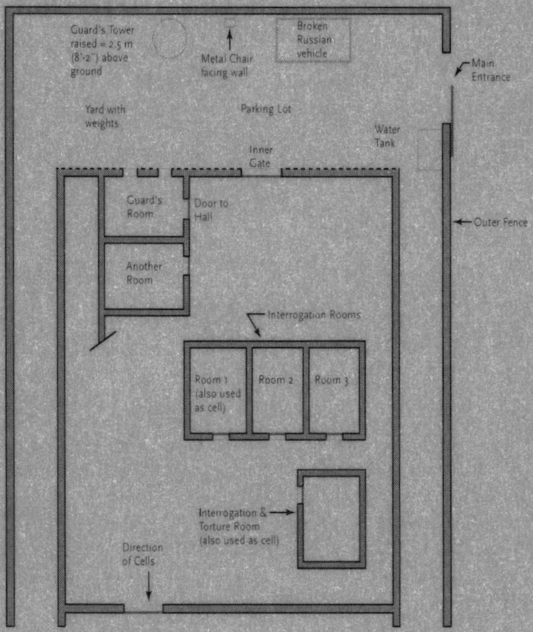

Guard's Tower raised ≈ 2.5 m (8'-2") above ground
Metal Chair facing wall
Broken Russian vehicle
Main Entrance
Yard with weights
Parking Lot
Water Tank
Inner Gate
Guard's Room
Door to Hall
Outer Fence
Another Room
Interrogation Rooms
Room 1 (also used as cell)
Room 2
Room 3
Interrogation & Torture Room (also used as cell)
Direction of Cells

Black Site (Exhibit M)

the doctor with the disfigured

hand shined a light on me

noted my marks

on a diagram of the human body

the doctor told me I was going

to a better "place"

A Toast (for Nawal Nasrallah)

Chair legs screech across the banquet floor
    above us, a wedding feast
of people pulling themselves closer, closer
    to the constellation of tables

while here underground, alone with our ears,
    we can't get close enough
to Al-Azzawi reciting "A Toast," and laughter
    in two languages marinates

the hunger of this room, and now you lean
    to hear him, who has not lived
in your homeland for most of his days on earth,
    like you who have lived

your country in kitchens, far from your country,
    testing the tastes of the ancients,
citizen of this implacable state and its armies
    pitching their permanent tent

in the dictator's palaces; you, who out of grief's
    maw, the daily shipwreck of news,
translate the alien clay of cuneiform relief
    into Mesopotamian stews,

a toast to you, Nawal, at whose Mesopotamian
    table I have been honored to sit
and be sated, not with fried eggplant but *buran*,
    not with drumsticks baked in fig

but with *Afkhadh al-Dijaj bil-Teen*, your homeland
transfigured by flame, Baghdad
now spiced with coriander, now stewed in the skin,
a toast to you, for my insides

still sing, and now the people above us are dancing,
they cannot help themselves,
they are wrapping themselves in a song,
stuffed like grape leaves,

they have no room for us in the light, so below
in our rootcellar of words,
here in the underland of exile, a toast to you,
the country of your tongue.

Cell/(ph)one (A simultaneity in four voices)

Instructions for use:

Tear out these pages, then cut into four columns for four readers. Have the readers perform their monologues simultaneously, reading through the text twice. Read line breaks as slight pauses, space breaks as silences. Improvisation is welcome.

1. [Cell/phone]

You are wanted. You are not
alone. You are wanted. You
are not alone.

Someone needs to answer
me now. Someone needs me
to answer now. Someone
needs me alone and no one
one else to answer now.

A watch. A phone. I watch.
I wait for you. For you alone.
I text. I cell. I tower above
alone. I sat alight, I roam
and charge this self own.

I am wanted. I have to take
this call. I have to take this
call. I have to take this call.
I have to take this call.

(repeat)

2. [Breaking Convo]

Hello?
Hey—
How ARE you?
You WHAT?
Huh? [Hold up finger]

What's up?
What? Hold on.
Say it again.

What's up?
What? [Turn head away]
Hold on. Hold on.
Say it again.
NO!!!
NO!!! NO!!! Oh hell no!
Yes, I can hold.

(repeat)

3. [Guantanamo]

Please pass this on to my wife.
Tell her it's time for her

to move on. I will never leave
Guantanamo. She must understand

I'm not abandoning her. That I
love her. But she must move on

with her life. She is getting older.
But I will never leave

Guantanamo. That I love her.
But she must move on
with her life.

(repeat)

4. [Intercept Message]

The number you have reached
has been disconnected.
If you need help, hang
up and dial the operator.

Please hang up and try again.

The following tones are for
the deaf community.

Dilililiiililillliliiiiilli

The number you have reached
has been disconnected.

Please hang up and try again.

Da da da da da da
Da da da da da da

(repeat)

v.

homefront/removes

A Narrative of the Renditions

of

Mohamad Farag Ahmad Bashmilah

) (

I hear it, at times, even in the wind. Black helicopters chut overhead, catch in the throat of leaden sky. They are watching. You are watching. Ache of eyes after staring at papers—the same tired arguments, the same disembodied I's. Sometimes it feels like drowning in my own skull. Rainwater leaking in the hall, thoughts of thighs at a funeral. They are watching, you are watching. I wrote nothing. I had nothing to say. Outside, unbutton your shirt. Handle each button as if attached by a single thread. Inside, the wind knocks over a powerline. Outside, unzip your pants so the zipper purrs. Inside, protesters gather at the embassy. Slip off underwear as if lost in thought. Outside, climb into bed as if it were filled with spiders. Inside, they are watching. I hear it.

) (

was taken was rapidly

cut off my blind

-fold was taken

off and strong light

beams on my eye

Case 5:07-cv-JW

Document 53

hand over my ___

diaper like a baby

my ears with spongy

and taped all around

headphones they put

dressing like you

would on a wound

over my eyes

) (

What consequence is a body. And if the eye were a lamp. In the beginning, there was a certain darkness, an uncertain darkness after. I'm trying to piece together something resembling the sea, in the frail moments before squall. For passengers to safely reach the stable osmotic. In the sudden wake, how to see the difference between "or" & "and"—on which matters of matter & spirit hang. If the eye. If a body a body none/theless loved by anons & disappeared. If a body separate & how. MOHAMED v. JEPPESEN, Inc. *Jeppesen: Transforming the Way the World Moves*. If I the see, sea again. What consequence is a body a body nonetheless. If the light in me is gone. Thus I the Doctor with Disfigured. Thus I, Scribe of Black Hives. If my body full of darkness.

)(

tried hanging myself

with string I pulled

out of my blanket

this chain had 24

links in it tried by

swallowing pills I was

this chain had 110

third time I slashed my wrists

the doctor with disfigured

hand who shined a light

my head against the wall

I trying to lose

a diagram of the body

myself by concentrating

on the smallest details

)(

I was planning my lesson on imagery, Introduction to Poetry. How Tu Fu said, it's like being alive twice. We were to read "The Colonel." My phone rang. *Have you heard?* Something about a plane crash. I could not understand. It was my first week in the Ivory Tower. But I had a plan and I had to go through with it. It's being a lie twice. *The moon swung bare on its black cord over the house.* How is this true? Any abstraction can lead to murder. I had to stop at every sentence so I did not weep. They didn't understand the first thing—how it's more like a building than a dream, more like a plane than a cloud. And you can enter it. I didn't understand the first thing. The second thing I stood. To find a set of unfamiliar keys. To open like the ear, when eye is shut.

) (

taken to outside court

yard to sit on metal

chair facing wall

guards would remove

my hood and stand behind

Case 5:07-cv-02798-JW

two-meter-high wall

would give me nail

clippers so I could cut

anything except the wall

could hear planes taking

off and landing

children's voices

outside the wall in

a language I believe

) (

In the wake of. I don't even speak the language. In glances and glares. *My son, you are Arab, be proud of it*, my Dad would say. I awaken. I avoid pulling up beside flagged trucks. Of ire I sing, mirror. Who turns to see me, the invisible now visible. Who lives in a want ad for a criminal act. *Fits the ethnicity, if you know what I mean*, my colleague said. Myself as numb stranger. *My son, you are Arab, be proud of it.* I count turned heads, raised eyebrows at the faculty meeting, when two Muslims are introduced as visiting professors in physics. What does it matter where numbers come from? B's father is still missing. Whose face, he'd joke, he never knew, seeing it was always behind a home movie camera. *My son*, I caught myself saying to no one who exists, *I am air.*

)(

I suspended upside

down from the ceiling

when I could no longer

feel they lowered me

a long chain clasped

to a leather belt around

ankles a piece of meat

pushed and let me spin

and lifted into the

air hanging me there

their beating would not leave

permanent marks

) (

You look at me / looking at you. How close the words *creation* and *cremation*. How in Hebrew, Adam is kin to *dust*, how the stars swam in Abraham's eyes, his profligate future. Uncountable windows of light, flashing open-eyed. The towers burned down into themselves—*just like a cigarette*, the poet laureate wanted to say, and did, on air, knowing that distance makes metaphors terrifying and the world less so, dividing the night from night. How to describe the twisted angles and planes? Picasso: *a picture is a sum of destructions.* The wind draws dust into us. Thus, E— who held klieg lights at Ground Zero carries the towers in lung roots. A kind of seeding, this seeing. We are windows, half-open, half-reflecting, trying to impersonate someone who can breathe.

) (

so I could pass the time

they also gave me

a Rubik's cube

p. 43 of 62

Case 5:07-cv-02798-JW

filled with water

another room filled

with water

& always under light

) (

As if, somehow, I were responsible. *Patriotism is a feeling,* the student wrote, *that is rotted deep inside every one of us, and it's hard to let something such as your country go to shame.* The photos of hijackers looked like a Warhol of our family album (the women oddly absent), portraits bleared in displaced layers of ink. Who fed you, who changed you, who memorized your hands, who breathed you in? The ex-editor of *Life* lays down the *old rule of thumb* in journalism: *one person dead in your paper's hometown equals five dead the next town over equals fifty dead in the next state or 5,000 dead in China.* The homeland is late blue, and tastes of metal, like blood in the mouth. My cousins my demons my plotting and foiled selves, what have you done, what have we done with us?

<hover to see video>

in another room another / while my wife and sick mother

used my blood to write / on the walls of / white

noise chaining the day / to day / imitate a donkey's bray

mattress and camera above the / the doctor revealed to me

to lose memory (unsay?) / "raping them would be the best way"

vacationing with family in Washington / "forget Jordan"

Nestlé bottles filled with water / in another room another

window the size of a computer / while my wife and sick mother

tried to compose myself (cell?) / an opening in the wall (well?)

express mail to Indonesia / another room another

speaking Pashto / the blanket black and "Made in Mexico"

plastic cups checked blue and red / number 00 33 on the inside

light constantly / while my wife and sick / red carpet behind me

they said Washington Washington / contrary information

in another room in another / room another in / another

) (

On the flight overseas, the rows dotted with isolatos, each an island of eyes. I was looking (for), looking (like). Ivan Zhdanov: *what outside is a cross, inside is a window.* A white woman across the aisle eyed me the entire flight. Her gaze widened and neck craned as I (her eyes) slowly removed (her eyes) my shoes. What could I say? Sometimes I'm afraid I'm carrying a bomb. That I'm a sleeper and don't know when I'll awaken. I should have said: Identity isn't an end—it's a portal, a deportation from the country of mirrors, an inflection within a question, punctuation in the sentence of birth. I said nothing. Later, visiting a Quaker meeting, I sat among scattered chairs. On the shores of breathing, all eyes shut, I waded. Silence our rudder, silence our harbor.

) (

I did not know my

exact moment of transfer

Case 5:07-dv-02798-JW

Filed 12/14/2007

I could tell by the smells

and sounds I was home

Page 53 of 62

my wife my children

attached hereto is a true

detained in Aden

and accurate rendering

constantly dizzy nose bleeds

like floating on water

I believe these things

happened because I had not

had not because I had not

been in the sun and was now

accurate rendering and was now

abundant sun

Compline

That we await a blessed hope, & that we will be struck
With great fear, like a baby taken into the night, that every boot,

Every improvised explosive, Talon & Hornet, Molotov
& rubber-coated bullet, every unexploded cluster bomblet,

Every Kevlar & suicide vest & unpiloted drone raining fire
On wedding parties will be burned as fuel in the dark season.

That we will learn the awful hunger of God, the nerve-fraying
Cry of God, the curdy vomit of God, the soiled swaddle of God,

The constant wakefulness of God, alongside the sweet scalp
Of God, the contented murmur of God, the limb-twitched dream-

Reaching of God. We're dizzy in every departure, limb-lost.
We cannot sleep in the wake of God, & God will not sleep

The infant dream for long. We lift the blinds, look out into ink
For light. My God, my God, open the spine binding our sight.

Notes

Sand Opera began out of the vertigo of feeling unheard as an Arab American, in the decade after the terrorist attacks of 2001. After 9/11, Americans turned an ear to the voices of Arabs and Muslims, though often it has been a fearful or selective listening. Even Errol Morris chose to interview only Americans for his Abu Ghraib film, "Standard Operating Procedure." After 9/11, I've found myself split—between my American upbringing and my Arab roots, between raising young children and witnessing the War on Terror abroad. I continue to ask myself what it means to be a human being—and what it means to rear vulnerable creatures—in a world where humans seem hell-bent on violence, using "defense" and "security" as alibis for domination and revenge. I take solace in Herodotus's notion of writing "to prevent these deeds from drifting into oblivion," and find peace in the durability of art—that momentary stay against confusion.

"Illumination of the Martyrdom of St. Bartholomew" is inspired by a manuscript leaf torn from a Laudario, which appeared in a visiting exhibition at the Cleveland Museum of Art.

"abu ghraib arias" is a dialogue between Standard Operation Procedure for Camp Delta in Guantanamo Bay, the soldiers who served in Abu Ghraib, and the Abu Ghraib prisoners. I draw upon a number of sources: a Standard Operating Procedure manual for Camp Echo at the Guantanamo Bay prison camp (thanks to WikiLeaks); the testimony of Abu Ghraib torture victims found in Mark Danner's *Torture and Truth: America, Abu Graib, and the War on Terror*; the words of U.S. soldiers and contractors as found in Philip Gourevitch and Errol Morris's *The Ballad of Abu Ghraib*; the official reports on the Abu Ghraib prison scandal (the Taguba Report, the Schlesinger Report, etc.); interviews with Joe Darby and Eric Fair (two whistle-blowers); the Bible; and the Code of Hammurabi.

"*Woman Mourning Son*" is inspired by a 2007 photograph by Alaa Al-Marjani.

"Recipe from the Abbasid" is inspired by an Abbasid recipe from Nawal Nasrallah's *Delights from the Garden of Eden: A Cookbook and History of the Iraqi Cuisine*.

"Home Sweet Home" relies upon a letter from a friend and an interview of a widow taken by Jim Sheeler and published in *Final Salute: A Story of Unfinished Lives*.

"The Iraqi Curator's PowerPoint" is for Donny George Youkhanna, the curator of the National Museum of Iraq during the invasion of Iraq. He died in 2011.

"Asymmetries" is after Spencer Tunick, and dedicated to Amy Breau.

"Salaam Epigrams" is inspired by the calligraphy of Nihad Dukhan and dedicated to Leila. Thanks to Nihad Dukhan for his permission to reprint in miniature his "salaam."

"War Stories" relies on a story shared by Rob Slattery, about a friend's brother who kept a box of ears from his time in Vietnam during the war.

"Hung Lyres" is for my daughters, Adele and Leila. The section "in the cell of else" refers to the interrogation of Mohamedou Ould Slahi at Guantanamo, who was exposed to "variable light patterns and music"—including Drowning Pool's "Let the Bodies Hit the Floor," "Barney Is a Dinosaur," Rage Against the Machine, and the *Sesame Street* theme.

"Breathing Together" relies on a letter from a friend.

"Testimony" is for Daniel Heyman, in gratitude for his documentary art on the testimonies of Iraqis.

"When I was a Child, I Lived as a Child, I Said to My Dad" is for Dad and Mom. It references a post-Gulf War video game, *The Mother of All Tank Battles*.

"Etruscan Cista Handle" describes a piece at the Cleveland Museum of Art, a 4th century cista handle.

"A Toast (for Nawal Nasrallah)" is for the exiles, especially Nawal Nasrallah, Shakir Mustafa, Kadhim Shaaban, and Salih Altoma.

On page 69, the image of Saddam Hussein's fingerprints can be found here: http://www2.gwu.edu/~nsarchiv/NSAEBB/NSAEBB279/ (National Security Archive, posted July 1, 2009, last accessed September 22, 2014).

"Cell/(ph)one (A simultaneity in four voices)" employs found language, including text from a story in the *New York Times* about a Guantanamo prisoner.

"Homefront/Removes" is dedicated to the victims of the terror war, especially to Mohamed Farag Ahmad Bashmilah, held and tortured in secret U.S. prisons. Bashmilah's legal case against Jeppesen Dataplan, a Boeing subsidiary, was for its knowing participation in the "extraordinary renditions" of detainees in the War on Terror. Throughout the book, one can find renderings of drawings by Bashmilah. His testimony is in italics.

"Compline" takes its name from the final prayer in the Book of Hours, which takes place late in the night. The poem borrows language from Isaiah.

Book Benefactors

Alice James Books wishes to thank the following individuals who generously contributed toward the publication of *Sand Opera*:

Kazim Ali
Nina Nyhart

For more information about AJB's book benefactor program, contact us via phone or email, or visit alicejamesbooks.org to see a list of forthcoming titles.

Recent Titles from Alice James Books

Devil, Dear, Mary Ann McFadden
Eros Is More, Juan Antonio González Iglesias, Translated by Curtis Bauer
Mad Honey Symposium, Sally Wen Mao
Split, Cathy Linh Che
Money Money Money | Water Water Water, Jane Mead
Orphan, Jan Heller Levi
Hum, Jamaal May
Viral, Suzanne Parker
We Come Elemental, Tamiko Beyer
Obscenely Yours, Angelo Nikolopoulos
Mezzanines, Matthew Olzmann
Lit from Inside: 40 Years of Poetry from Alice James Books, Edited by Anne Marie Macari and Carey Salerno
Black Crow Dress, Roxane Beth Johnson
Dark Elderberry Branch: Poems of Marina Tsvetaeva, A Reading by Ilya Kaminsky and Jean Valentine
Tantivy, Donald Revell
Murder Ballad, Jane Springer
Sudden Dog, Matthew Pennock
Western Practice, Stephen Motika
me and Nina, Monica A. Hand
Hagar Before the Occupation | Hagar After the Occupation, Amal al-Jubouri
Pier, Janine Oshiro
Heart First into the Forest, Stacy Gnall
This Strange Land, Shara McCallum
lie down too, Lesle Lewis
Panic, Laura McCullough
Milk Dress, Nicole Cooley
Parable of Hide and Seek, Chad Sweeney
Shahid Reads His Own Palm, Reginald Dwayne Betts
How to Catch a Falling Knife, Daniel Johnson

Alice James Books has been publishing poetry since 1973. The press was founded in Boston, Massachusetts as a cooperative wherein authors performed the day-to-day undertakings of the press. This collaborative element remains viable even today, as authors who publish with the press are also invited to become members of the editorial board and participate in editorial decisions at the press. The editorial board selects manuscripts for publication via the press's annual, national competition, the Alice James Award. Alice James Books seeks to support women writers and was named for Alice James, sister to William and Henry, whose extraordinary gift for writing went unrecognized during her lifetime.

Designed by Mary Austin Speaker

Printed by BookMobile